Forever Grateful To You:

Made in the USA
Middletown, DE
29 June 2022

68000178R00062